# Challenge Your Child

## A Rainbow of Mind-Bending Experiences for the Third Grader

### By Becky Daniel

Cover Design
by Terri Moll

Inside Illustrations
by Tim Foley

Published by Instructional Fair • TS Denison
an imprint of

 McGraw-Hill
Children's Publishing

## About the Author

Becky Daniel is a parent, teacher, author, and editor. After graduating from California University at Long Beach, she taught kindergarten through eighth grade. She left the classroom after the birth of her first daughter to care for her child and to pursue a career in writing at home. Now the mother of three, Becky edits a magazine and writes educational books from her home in Orcutt, California. Over the past 25 years, she has written more than 200 educational resource books, including several titles for Instructional Fair • TS Denison.

## Credits

Author .................................................Becky Daniel
Inside Illustrations................................Tim Foley
Cover Design.........................................Terri Moll
Cover Photograph ...............................© Stockbyte
Page and Icon Design...........................Mark Conrad
Project Director ....................................Kelly Morris Huxmann
Editors .................................................Kelly Morris Huxmann, Linda Triemstra
Classroom Consultant .........................Janice Hass

*McGraw-Hill*
*Children's Publishing*

*A Division of The McGraw·Hill Companies*

Published by Instructional Fair • TS Denison
An imprint of McGraw–Hill Children's Publishing
Copyright © 2000 McGraw–Hill Children's Publishing

Send all inquiries to:
McGraw–Hill Children's Publishing
3195 Wilson Drive NW
Grand Rapids, Michigan 49544

*Challenge Your Child—Grade 3*
ISBN: 0-7424-0040-9

# Table of Contents

# Introduction

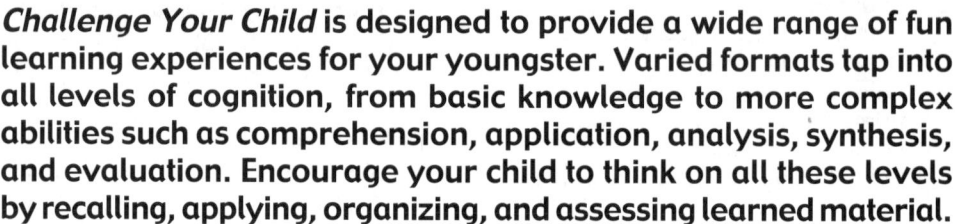

*Challenge Your Child* is designed to provide a wide range of fun learning experiences for your youngster. Varied formats tap into all levels of cognition, from basic knowledge to more complex abilities such as comprehension, application, analysis, synthesis, and evaluation. Encourage your child to think on all these levels by recalling, applying, organizing, and assessing learned material.

Take an active role in your child's learning. Guide your child through the activities in this book, focusing on those that are best suited for him or her. *Reluctant readers may need help reading directions in order to complete some activities.* Use the activities as a springboard for further investigations. The level of interest you show will serve to increase your child's own motivation.

You will see one very important icon throughout this book. This sign appears on pages that require adult permission, supervision, or other assistance. Be sure your child understands the importance of asking for help in completing these activities.

An answer key is provided in the center of the book for easy self-checking. Simply straighten the staples to remove the pages, then fold the staples again to keep the remainder of the book intact.

# Jungle Safari

analysis

Find and color the fifteen animals hidden in the jungle.

## Can you identify each animal below?

| | | |
|---|---|---|
| 1. jaguar | 6. macaw | 11. manatee |
| 2. tarantula | 7. iguana | 12. toucan |
| 3. monkey | 8. tree frog | 13. sloth |
| 4. giant anteater | 9. butterfly | 14. bat |
| 5. boa constrictor | 10. alligator | 15. ant |

analysis

# The Birthday Party

Find and circle twelve things wrong with this picture.

# Colorful Words

application

Color each word below to give it a special meaning. Example: Color the word "bird" blue to make a blue-bird. Think carefully before coloring!

House

Whale     Hole

Jacket     Mail

E     Berry

Head     V

comprehension

# Homonym Hunt

> *Homonyms* are words that sound the same but have different meanings. They may or may not be spelled the same. List homonym pairs to fit the clues below.

1. a color & what the wind did yesterday

_____     _____

2. a color & what you did with a book yesterday

_____     _____

3. part of your foot & getting well

_____     _____

4. to look & the ocean

_____     _____

5. to complete & moisture on the ground

_____     _____

6. letters in envelopes & a man

_____     _____

7. something in the sky & a mother's boy child

_____     _____

8. when something is equal & a place with rides

_____     _____

**Brain Booster:** List as many sets of homonyms as you can.

IF0294 *Challenge Your Child*

# What Fits Both?

analysis

In each box, draw something that both words describe.

| | |
|---|---|
| **big and loud** | **sour and juicy** |
| **hungry and wet** | **fuzzy and green** |
| **big and soft** | **hot and sweet** |
| **tiny and soft** | **dangerous and alive** |

# Color Sense

evaluation

Imagine you could smell, hear, taste, or feel colors. Complete the chart with the first words that come to your mind.

| | aroma | sound | taste | texture |
|---|---|---|---|---|
| red | smoky | | | |
| blue | | flute | | |
| yellow | | | sour | |
| green | | | | |
| purple | | | | |
| orange | | | | |
| brown | | | | |
| black | | | | |
| white | | | | |

IF0294 *Challenge Your Child*

# Holiday Seasons

evaluation

When do people celebrate these holidays? Draw a check mark under the correct season for each holiday.

| | winter | spring | summer | autumn |
|---|---|---|---|---|
| Earth Day | | | | |
| Boxing Day | | | | |
| Kwanzaa | | | | |
| Groundhog Day | | | | |
| Grandparents Day | | | | |
| Cinco de Mayo | | | | |
| Flag Day | | | | |
| Rosh Hashanah | | | | |
| Presidents' Day | | | | |
| Martin Luther King, Jr. Day | | | | |
| St. Patrick's Day | | | | |
| Labor Day | | | | |

Circle the holidays that you and your family celebrate.

IF0294 *Challenge Your Child*

synthesis

# Make Your Own Tangram

Make your own sturdy tangram. Trace the pattern below onto white paper. Glue onto poster board, then cut out the pieces carefully. You may also choose to laminate the pieces using clear contact paper.

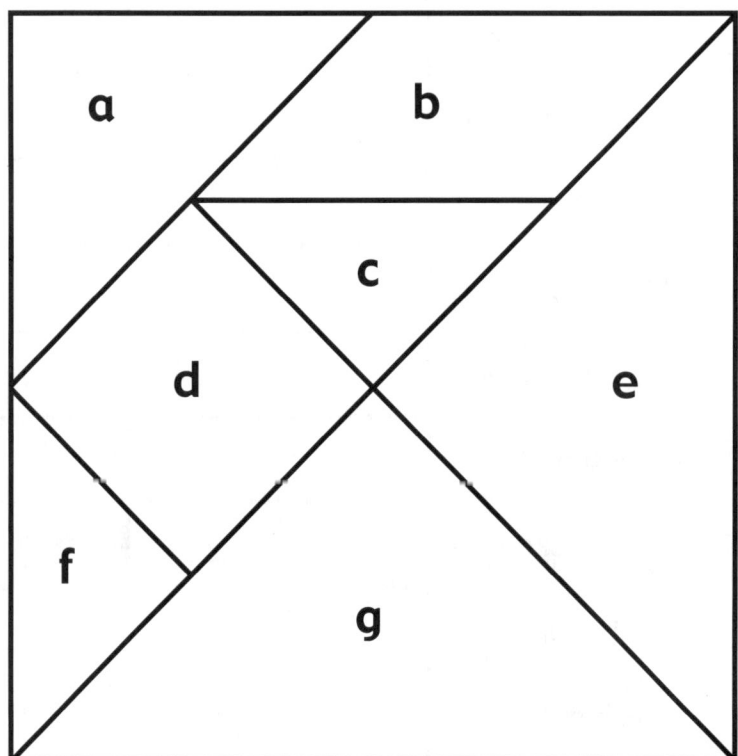

Can you arrange your tangram pieces to create the shapes below?

IF0294 *Challenge Your Child*

# Tangram Animals

synthesis

Write the correct letter to answer each riddle. Then try to create the animal shapes using your tangram pieces.

_____ 1. I can run very fast. My home is called a "burrow."

_____ 2. A group of animals like me is called a "school."

_____ 3. I can store water and carry it with me.

_____ 4. I often fly in circles before eating.

_____ 5. I am a clever animal. My babies are called "kits."

_____ 6. I often chase cars and like to bury things.

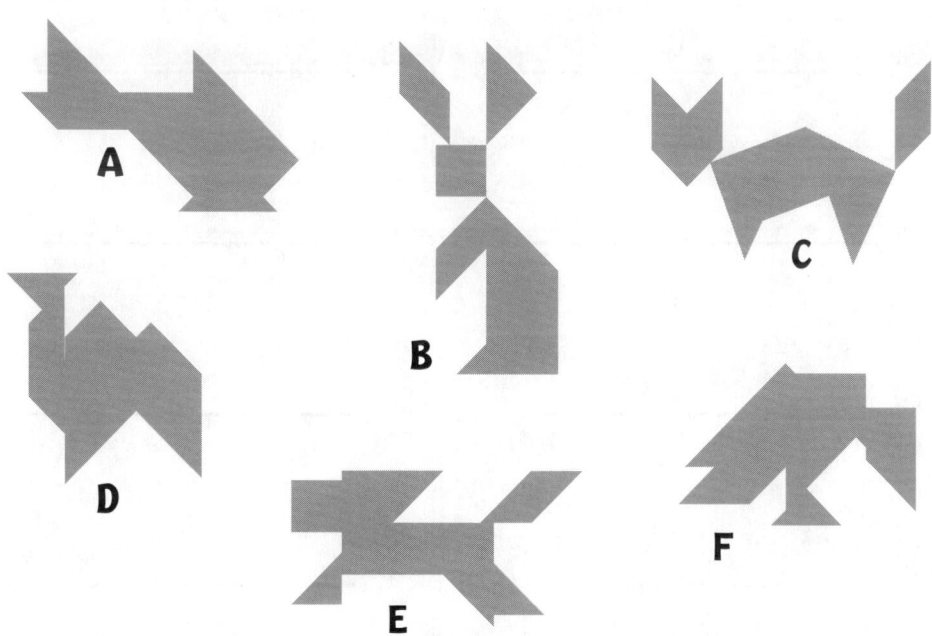

A

B

C

D

E

F

Create other animals with your tangram pieces.
Draw them on another sheet of paper.

synthesis

# Popping Good Ideas

Can you think of creative uses for popcorn? Fold this page in half along the dotted line. List six unique ideas for using popcorn in the left column. Then ask a friend to do the same in the right column without looking at your answers. Compare your ideas.

1. _____

2. _____

3. _____

4. _____

5. _____

6. _____

1. _____

2. _____

3. _____

4. _____

5. _____

6. _____

# Vanishing Vowels

comprehension

Fill in the vowels to name twenty different animals.

1. __ __ r d v __ r k

2. v __ l t __ r e

3. w i l d __ b __ __ s t

4. __ __ l

5. j __ c k __ l

6. l __ __ c h

7. l l __ m __

8. c h __ n c h __ l l a

9. c __ n __ r y

10. p __ n d __

11. b __ r r __ c u d __

12. c __ y __ t e

13. w __ l l __ b y

14. m __ c __ w

15. __ l p __ c __

16. p r __ n g h __ r n

17. s n __ w y __ w l

18. b __ __ t l __

19. __ g r __ t

20. m __ n g __ __ s e

# In Search of Nouns

A *noun* can be a person, place, or thing. Find fifteen nouns in the puzzle below. You will find the words hidden horizontally and vertically.

```
Y  B  A  S  T  R  O  N  A  U  T
R  E  S  T  A  U  R  A  N  T  T
U  I  C  M  T  E  A  C  H  E  R
N  C  H  I  L  D  X  A  V  O  E
C  F  O  B  E  J  G  R  L  M  E
L  R  O  E  S  F  A  R  I  O  W
E  P  L  A  Y  G  R  O  U  N  D
S  T  O  R  E  N  A  T  S  K  A
I  P  A  N  T  S  G  P  O  E  H
Q  U  S  I  S  T  E  R  V  Y  N
```

List each noun you find under the correct category.

| Person | Place | Thing |
|--------|-------|-------|
| _____ | _____ | _____ |
| _____ | _____ | _____ |
| _____ | _____ | _____ |
| _____ | _____ | _____ |
| _____ | _____ | _____ |

# Elephant Jokes

application

The great thing about elephant jokes is they don't have to make sense! Write a punch line for each joke below. Remember: there are no wrong answers.*

1. Why did the elephant paint its toenails red?

   _____

2. How do you know when there is an elephant under your bed?

   _____

3. What do you call an elephant that flies?

   _____

4. What do you get if you cross an elephant and a kangaroo?

   _____

5. How does an elephant get down from a tree?

   _____

6. Why were the elephants thrown out of the swimming pool?

   _____

7. What time is it when an elephant sits on the fence?

   _____

8. Why does an elephant wear sneakers?

   _____

**\* Some possible answers are given in the answer key.**

**17**

knowledge

# Blend Factory

Build words using a beginning from the first column and an ending from the second column. Write your words below. Can you create thirty-two different words?

| | |
|---|---|
| bl | ab |
| br | ack |
| cl | ad |
| cr | ain |
| dr | am |
| fl | ame |
| fr | ane |
| gl | eam |
| gr | eck |
| pl | eep |
| sn | eet |
| st | ing |
| str | ook |
| thr | ow |
| tr | uff |
| wr | um |

1. _____
2. _____
3. _____
4. _____
5. _____
6. _____
7. _____
8. _____
9. _____
10. _____
11. _____
12. _____
13. _____
14. _____
15. _____
16. _____

17. _____
18. _____
19. _____
20. _____
21. _____
22. _____
23. _____
24. _____
25. _____
26. _____
27. _____
28. _____
29. _____
30. _____
31. _____
32. _____

**Brain Booster:** Can you build twenty-five more words using these same letters?

18

# Antonym Art

comprehension

*Antonyms* are words that have opposite meanings. Draw an antonym for each word below.

ajar

**miserable**

**powerful**

**grotesque**

**wealthy**

**sharp**

**sickly**

**flexible**

**plain**

# Who? What? Where?

Words can describe who, what happened, and where.
Read each sentence below. Then answer who, what,
and where on the lines that follow each sentence.

1. The astronaut landed on the moon.
   Who? _____
   What? _____
   Where? _____

2. The newborn baby slept in a small basket.
   Who? _____
   What? _____
   Where? _____

3. The wild animals paced in locked cages.
   Who? _____
   What? _____
   Where? _____

4. My friend went to Hawaii last March.
   Who? _____
   What? _____
   Where? _____

5. A stranger slipped a note in Troy's pocket.
   Who? _____
   What? _____
   Where? _____

6. Santa kept his reindeer at the North Pole.
   Who? _____
   What? _____
   Where? _____

IF0294 *Challenge Your Child*

# Color Survey

analysis

Take a survey to find out if boys and girls have the same favorite colors. Ask six girls and six boys to name their favorite colors. Keep track using tally marks below. Then make two graphs like the one on this page—one for boys and one for girls. Fill in one space for each tally mark. Compare your graphs. What do you discover?

**Girls** _____  _____  _____  _____  _____  _____  _____

**Boys** _____  _____  _____  _____  _____  _____  _____

blue    green    orange    pink    purple    red    yellow

| | blue | green | orange | pink | purple | red | yellow |
|---|---|---|---|---|---|---|---|
| 6 | | | | | | | |
| 5 | | | | | | | |
| 4 | | | | | | | |
| 3 | | | | | | | |
| 2 | | | | | | | |
| 1 | | | | | | | |

blue    green    orange    pink    purple    red    yellow

**Just for Fun:** Choose another topic, such as favorite sports or favorite foods. Survey six boys and six girls. Graph your results.

**21**

# Smiling Similes

synthesis

A *simile* is a figure of speech that compares two things using either *as* or *like*. Draw cartoons to illustrate the similes below.

She sings like a bird.

He's thin as a rail.

The horse runs like lightning.

She's slow as a snail.

He's as angry as a storm.

She's as sharp as a tack.

Try writing your own similes on another sheet of paper.

IF0294 *Challenge Your Child*

# Phone Book Fun

knowledge

> Answer the first part of each question on your own.
> Then use a phone book to answer the second part.

1. Who lives right next door? _____

   What is his/her phone number? _____

2. What is the very first name listed in the phone book? _____

   What is that person's phone number? _____

3. What is the very last name listed in the phone book? _____

   What is that person's address? _____

4. Who is the first person with a last name beginning with "S" in your phone book? _____

   What is the person's phone number? _____

5. Who is the last person with a last name beginning with "M" in your phone book? _____

   What is the person's address? _____

# Line Design

synthesis

Create a line design. Use a ruler to draw a straight line between all the like numbers.

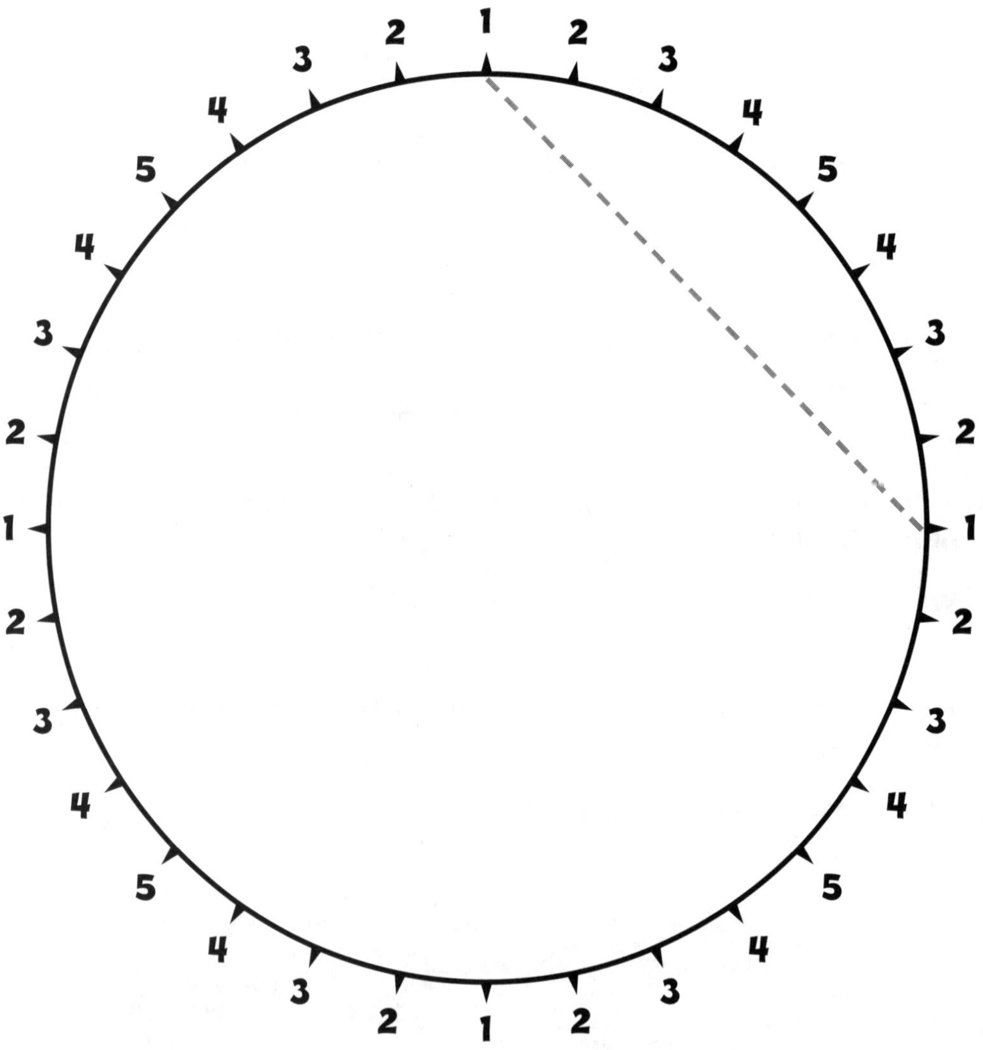

# Create Your Own Line Design

synthesis

Make your own unique line design. Write the numerals 1 through 4 around the circle in a repeated pattern such as 1-2-1-3-1-4 or 1-1-2-2-3-3-4-4. Use a ruler to connect all the same numbers. Color your design.

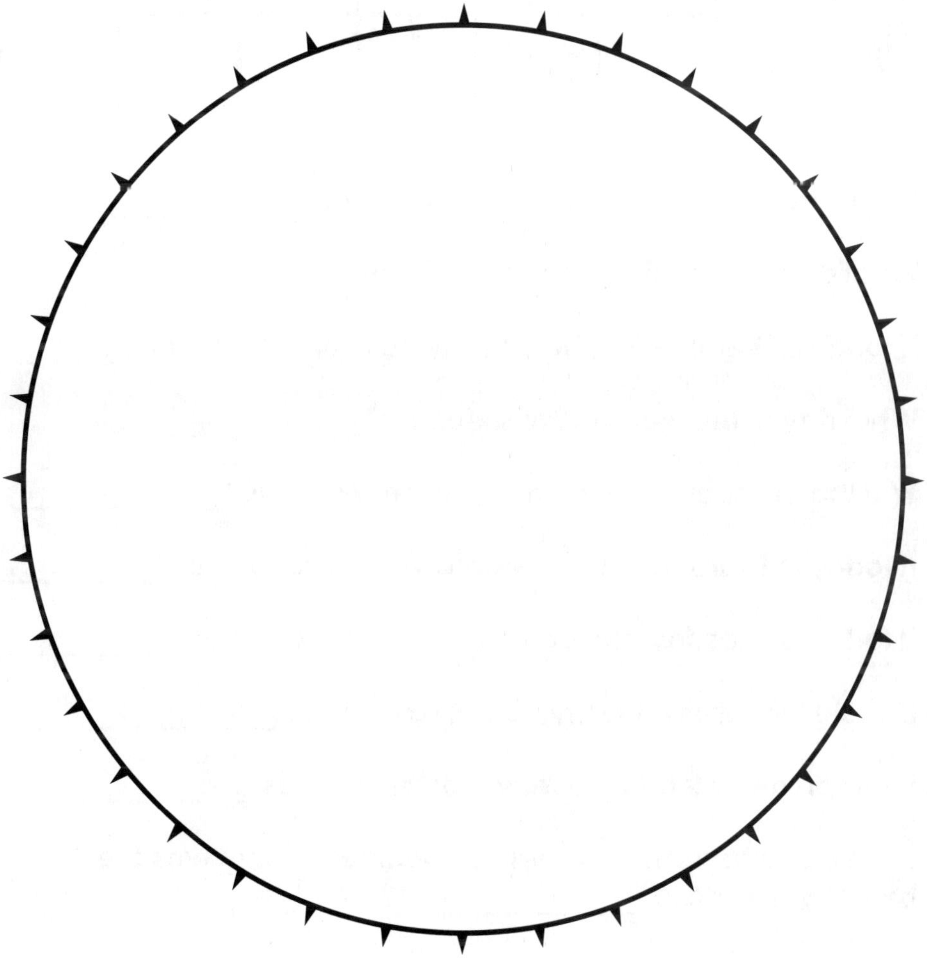

# Calendar Math

analysis

Use the partial calendar to answer the questions.

| Su | M | Tu | W | Th | F | Sa |
|----|----|----|----|----|----|----|
|    |    | 1  | 2  | 3  | 4  | 5  |
| 6  | 7  | 8  |    |    |    |    |

1. Will there be a Friday the 13th this month? _____

2. What date is the third Monday of the month? _____

3. If today is Wednesday, how many days until Monday? _____

4. What day of the week is the sixteenth? _____

5. Will the fourteenth fall on a Sunday or Monday? _____

6. If today is Thursday, the day before yesterday was _____.

7. If today is Tuesday, the day after tomorrow will be _____.

8. If yesterday was Monday, tomorrow will be _____.

9. If tomorrow will be Thursday, yesterday was _____.

10. If the day after tomorrow will be Saturday, what was the day before yesterday? _____

**Brain Booster:** Pretend the month is September. What day of the week is the last day of the month?

26

# Curious Coordinates

knowledge

Fill in the ordered pairs to answer the questions below.

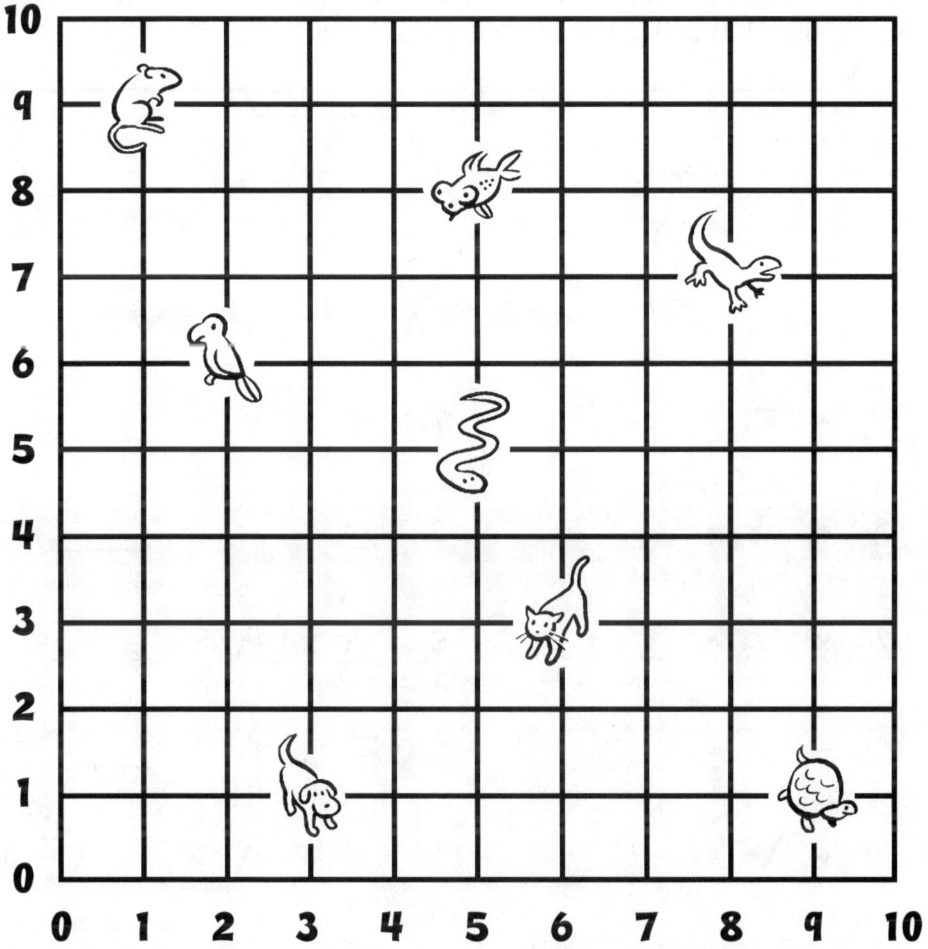

Where is the fish?     (   ,   )     Where is the puppy?   (   ,   )

Where is the snake?   (   ,   )     Where is the parrot?   (   ,   )

Where is the kitten?   (   ,   )     Where is the lizard?   (   ,   )

Which animal is at (1,9)? _____

Which animal is at (9,1)? _____

# Hexagon Math

analysis

Look at the secret number code. Do you see why /• = 6? Do you see why •̱ = 4? If not, study the code again, or ask an adult for help. Once you have cracked the code, use it to solve the problems below.

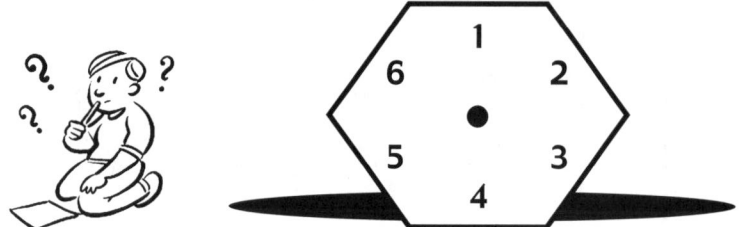

1. •̄ + •̄ = _____

2. •/ + •\ = _____

3. •/ x •/ = _____

4. •/ + •̱ = _____

5. •/ x \• = _____

6. •\ + •̱ = _____

7. \• x \• = _____

8. /• + /• = _____

9. •\ x •\ = _____

10. •̄ x •\ = _____

11. •̱ + •\ = _____

12. \• x •\ = _____

IF0294 *Challenge Your Child*

# Tic-Tac-Toe Math

analysis

Look at the secret number code. Do you see why ⌞ = 4 or why ⌐ = 12? If not, study the code again, or ask an adult for help. Once you have cracked the code, use it to solve the problems below.

| 2 | 3 | 4 |
|---|---|---|
| 5 | 6 | 8 |
| 9 | 10 | 12 |

1. ⌟ – ⌟ = _____

2. □ ÷ ⌟ = _____

3. ⌞ – ⌟ = _____

4. ⌐ – ⌞ = _____

5. □ ÷ ⊔ = _____

6. ⊓ ÷ ⊐ = _____

7. ⌐ ÷ ⌟ = _____

8. ⌐ – ⊔ = _____

9. ⌐ ÷ ⊔ = _____

10. ⊓ – ⌟ = _____

11. ⌐ ÷ ⌟ = _____

12. ⌐ ÷ ⌞ = _____

# Roll of the Dice

synthesis

**What is the most common total to roll with two dice?**

Draw all possible combinations for each total of the dice. Draw each combination only once. Example: Draw 5 & 6 OR 6 & 5, but not both. The first total has been done for you.

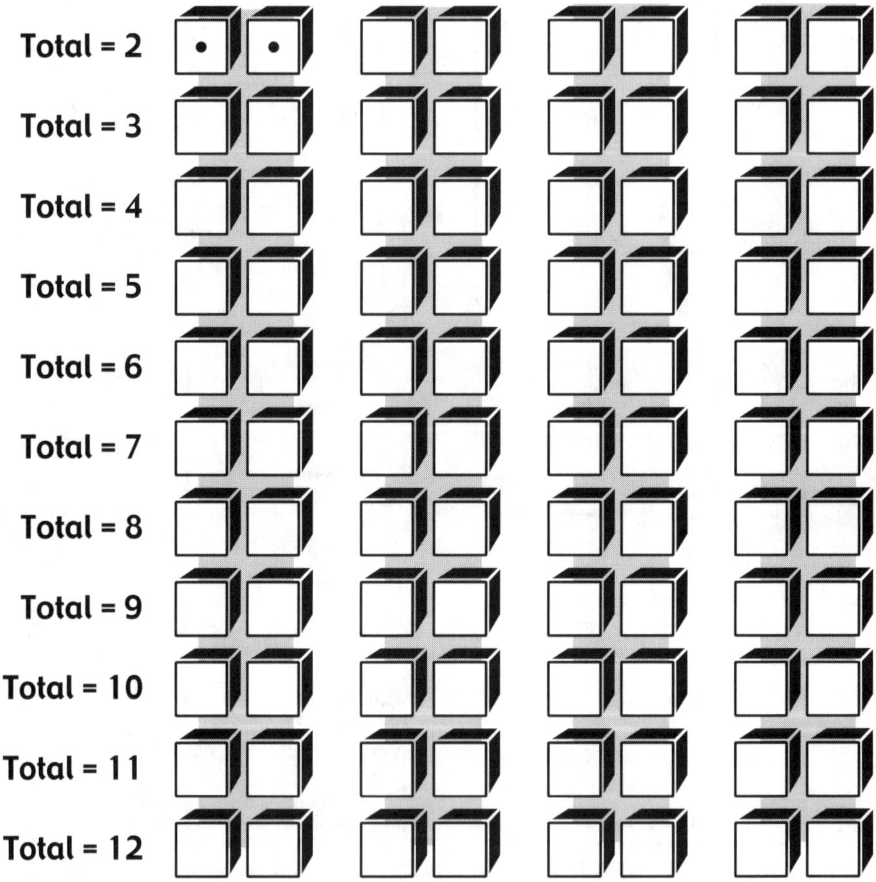

Total = 2

Total = 3

Total = 4

Total = 5

Total = 6

Total = 7

Total = 8

Total = 9

Total = 10

Total = 11

Total = 12

Draw a ⭐ next to the totals you think are easiest to roll. Then roll two dice 100 times. Keep track of the total for each roll using tally marks. Compare your results to the totals here.

IF0294 *Challenge Your Child*

# Numerical Path

knowledge

Starting at the number 1, trace a path through the maze.
Count by threes. Can you find your way to 100?

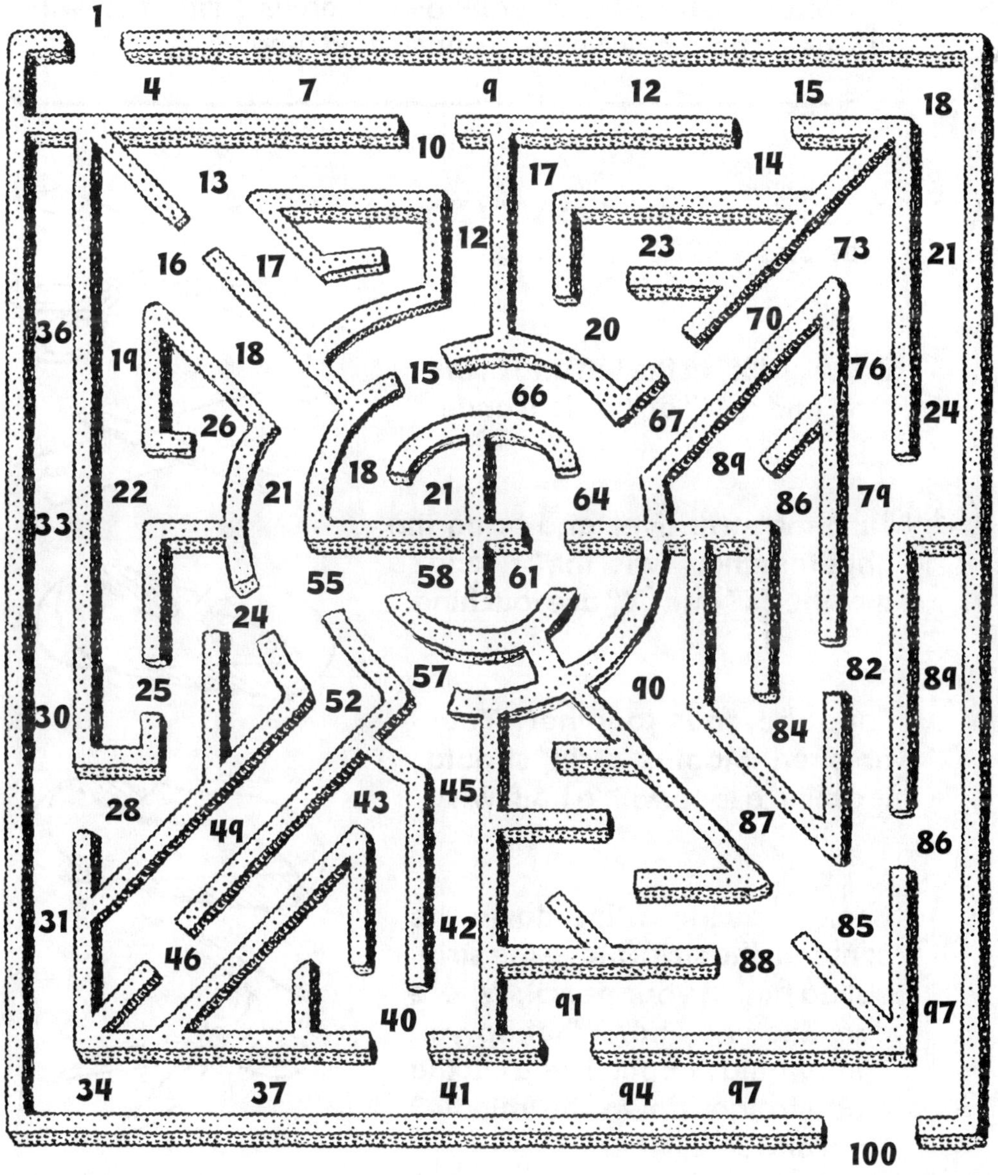

1

4          7          q          12          15
                                                    18
           10
13                    17              14
                                            73
16      17      12          23                21
                                        70
36              15              20      76
        18                  66
19              18      21          67      24
26                          64      8q
22      21                      86      79
33              58   61
        55
        24                              82      8q
25      57              q0
30              52              84
28      45          87          86
        4q      43                      85
31          42          88
        46              q1                  q7
34      37      41      q4      q7
                                    100

synthesis

# Mobius Strip

August Ferdinand Mobius was a German astronomer and mathematician born in 1790. He described the concept of infinity using a strip of paper later called the Mobius strip. Make your own Mobius strip. You will need: paper, scissors, a pencil, and tape.

**1** Cut a strip of paper that is 1" (25 mm) wide and 8" (200 mm) long.

**2** Draw an "X" at the left end of the strip and a "Y" at the right end.

**3** Turn the strip over and bring the ends together. Twist the "Y" end so that the "X" and "Y" are touching.

**4** Tape the ends together. Your finished Mobius strip should look like a loop with a half twist.

**5** Begin drawing a line down the center of the strip. Move the strip, but do not lift your pencil. Where does the line end? What do you think would happen if you cut the loop straight down the middle? Try it and see.

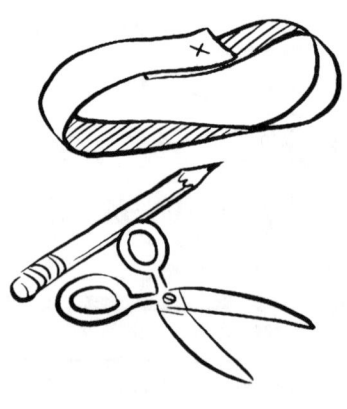

# A Magic Trick

synthesis

> Amaze friends and family with this magic number trick. You will need only the four boxes of numbers below, called A, B, C, and D.

1. Ask a friend to think of a number between one and fifteen.

2. Have your friend list every box in which the number appears.

3. "Guess" your friend's number. Here's how: Take the number directly below the letter of each box named and add. Example: If the number is in boxes A and B, add 1 + 2 = 3. It works every time.

| A | 5 | 11 |
|---|---|----|
| 1 | 7 | 13 |
| 3 | 9 | 15 |

| B | 6 | 11 |
|---|---|----|
| 2 | 7 | 14 |
| 3 | 10 | 15 |

| C | 6 | 13 |
|---|---|----|
| 4 | 7 | 14 |
| 5 | 12 | 15 |

| D | 10 | 13 |
|---|----|----|
| 8 | 11 | 14 |
| 9 | 12 | 15 |

33

synthesis

# The Greatest

Play this number game with a friend. You will need: one die and two copies of the score sheet below

**Objective:** Write the largest three-digit number possible.

**How to play:** Each game has eight rounds. For each round, roll the die three times. After each roll, write the number indicated on one of the three lines. The object is to write the largest three-digit number possible.

After eight rounds, add up your scores. For each round, the person who wrote the larger number receives one point. Score an additional two points for writing the greatest number possible in each round. If the score is tied, play a tiebreaker round to determine the winner. The winner is the player with more points.

Round 1: _____   _____   _____

Round 2: _____   _____   _____

Round 3: _____   _____   _____

Round 4: _____   _____   _____

Round 5: _____   _____   _____

Round 6: _____   _____   _____

Round 7: _____   _____   _____

Round 8: _____   _____   _____

Tiebreaker: _____   _____   _____

# The Next Number

Look for a pattern in each row of numbers. Follow the pattern to write the next three numbers on the lines.

1. ( 3    5    8    12 )          ____  ____  ____

2. ( 147    152    150    155 )          ____  ____  ____

3. ( 3    12    48    192 )          ____  ____  ____

4. ( 204    230    198    224 )          ____  ____  ____

5. ( 3    10    24    45 )          ____  ____  ____

6. ( 16    32    28    56 )          ____  ____  ____

7. ( 1,212    1,357    1,302    1,447 )          ____  ____  ____

8. ( 17    17    34    102 )          ____  ____  ____

IF0294 *Challenge Your Child*

analysis

# Marshmallow Madness

About how many miniature marshmallows will fit in a coffee mug? Take a guess. Then discover for yourself.

Fill a coffee mug with marshmallows, one handful at a time. Tap the bottom of the mug so the marshmallows settle. Continue until the mug is full. Once the mug is full, remove and count the marshmallows.

Use your marshmallows to answer the questions below.

1. Placed end to end, how long is a row of 100 miniature marshmallows? _____

2. Would it take more or less than a coffee mug of miniature marshmallows to build a chain 10" (25 cm) long? _____

3. How long does it take to melt a mug full of miniature marshmallows? _____ To find out, heat in microwave on **HIGH** for 10 seconds at a time.

**Just for Fun:** Add 1 cup (237 ml) crisped rice cereal or granola to 1 cup (237 ml) melted marshmallows. Stir. Pour onto a buttered plate and let sit for thirty minutes. Cut into pieces and serve.

IF0294 *Challenge Your Child*

# Flight Graph

synthesis

Make a paper airplane. Use the diagram below or your own design. Then take your airplane outside, along with a tape measure. Toss the plane ten times. Each time, record how far it traveled to the nearest yard or meter. Use the graph below to record each flight.

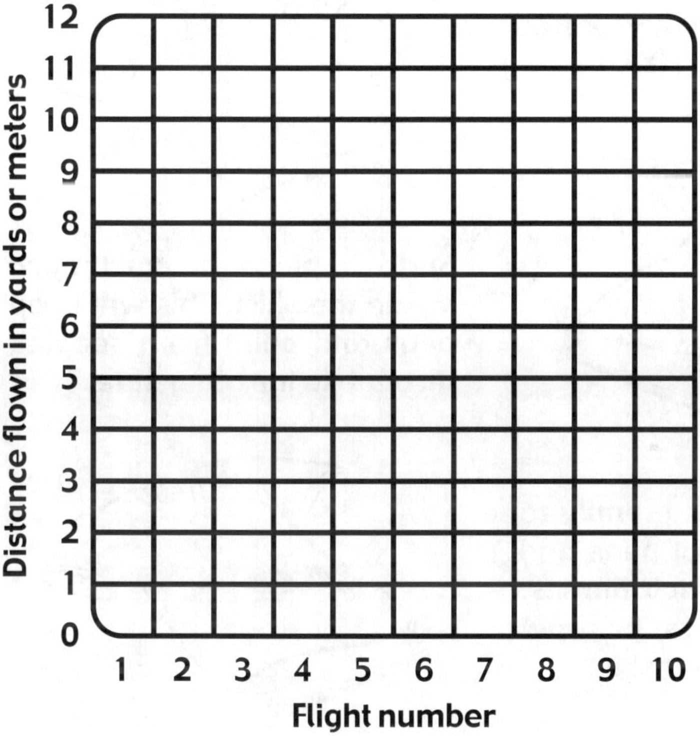

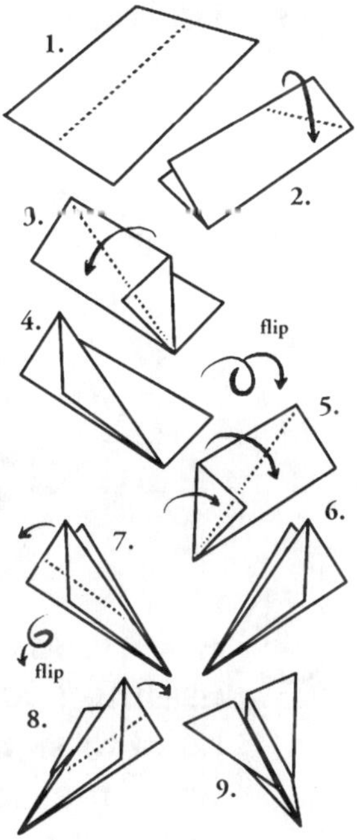

**Distance flown in yards or meters** (vertical axis: 0–12)

**Flight number** (horizontal axis: 1–10)

Use your graph to answer the following questions.

1. How far was the longest flight? _____

2. How far was the shortest flight? _____

3. What was the difference in distance between the two flights? _____

# Autographed Tee

synthesis

Create a T-shirt that your friends can autograph for you. You will need: one white or light-colored T-shirt, fabric marking pens or fabric paint, and a piece of heavy cardboard.

**1** Find a clean, light-colored T-shirt in your size.

**2** Slide a piece of cardboard inside the shirt. This will keep pens and paint from seeping through to the other side.

**3** Ask friends and family to use the special pens and paint to sign their names, write messages, or draw pictures on your shirt.

**4** Let the shirt dry thoroughly. Remove the cardboard and your shirt is ready to wear.

# Answer Key

## p. 5—Jungle Safari

## p. 6—The Birthday Party

## p. 8—Colorful Words
house (white or green)
whale (blue)
hole (black)
jacket (yellow)
mail (black)
E (brown)
berry (blue or black)
head (red)
V (gray)

## p. 8—Homonym Hunt
1. blue, blew
2. red, read
3. heel, heal
4. see, sea
5. do, dew
6. mail, male
7. sun, son
8. fair, fair

## p. 9—What Fits Both?
Answers will vary.

## p. 10—Color Sense
Answers will vary.

## p. 11—Holiday Seasons

|  | winter | spring | summer | autumn |
|---|---|---|---|---|
| Earth Day | | ✔ | | |
| Boxing Day | ✔ | | | |
| Kwanzaa | ✔ | | | |
| Groundhog Day | ✔ | | | |
| Grandparents Day | | | ✔ | |
| Cinco de Mayo | | ✔ | | |
| Flag Day | | ✔ | | |
| Rosh Hashanah | | | | ✔ |
| Presidents' Day | ✔ | | | |
| Martin Luther King, Jr. Day | ✔ | | | |
| St. Patrick's Day | ✔ | | | |
| Labor Day | | | ✔ | |

## p. 12—Make Your Own Tangram

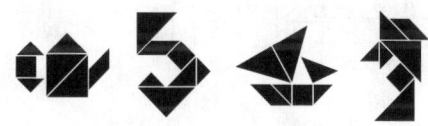

## p. 13—Tangram Animals
1. B
2. A
3. D
4. F
5. C
6. E

## p. 13 (continued)

## p. 14—Popping Good Ideas
Answers will vary.

## p. 15—Vanishing Vowels
1. aardvark
2. vulture
3. wildebeest
4. eel
5. jackal
6. leech
7. llama
8. chinchilla
9. canary
10. panda
11. barracuda
12. coyote
13. wallaby
14. macaw
15. alpaca
16. pronghorn
17. snowy owl
18. beetle
19. egret
20. mongoose

## p. 16—In Search of Nouns

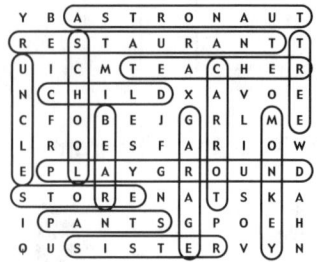

| Person | Place | Thing |
|---|---|---|
| astronaut | restaurant | pants |
| teacher | playground | bear |
| child | store | carrot |
| sister | school | monkey |
| uncle | garage | tree |

## p. 17—Elephant Jokes
Answers will vary.
1. So it could hide in an apple tree
2. When your nose touches the ceiling
3. A jumbo jet
4. Big holes in the ground
5. He uses a parachute
6. Because they couldn't keep up their trunks
7. Time to get a new fence
8. So it can run fast and sneak up on mice

## p. 18—Blend Factory

| | | | |
|---|---|---|---|
| blab | cream | gleam | steam |
| black | creep | glow | steep |
| blame | crook | glum | sting |
| bleep | crow | grab | stow |
| blow | drab | grain | stuff |
| bluff | drain | greet | strain |
| brad | dream | grow | stream |
| brain | dreck | gruff | street |
| bring | drum | plain | string |
| brook | flab | plane | strum |
| brow | flack | plow | throw |
| clack | flame | plum | track |
| clad | fleck | snack | train |
| clam | fleet | snow | tram |
| cling | fling | snuff | wrack |
| crab | flow | stab | wreck |
| crack | fluff | stack | wring |
| cram | frame | stain | |
| crane | glad | | |

## p. 19—Antonym Art
Pictures will vary.
miserable—happy
ajar—closed
powerful—weak
grotesque—beautiful
wealthy—poor
sharp—dull
sickly—healthy
flexible—stiff
plain—decorative, fancy

## p. 20—Who? What? Where?

1. Who? the astronaut
   What? landed
   Where? on the moon

2. Who? the newborn baby
   What? slept
   Where? in a small basket

3. Who? the wild animals
   What? paced
   Where? in locked cages

4. Who? my friend
   What? went
   Where? to Hawaii

5. Who? a stranger
   What? slipped a note
   Where? in Troy's pocket

6. Who? Santa
   What? kept his reindeer
   Where? at the North Pole

## p. 24—Line Design

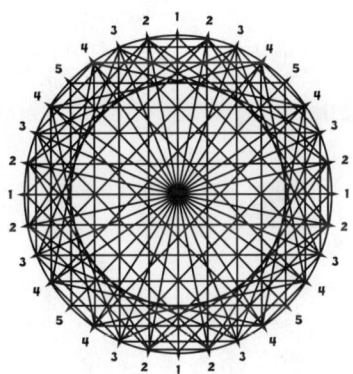

## p. 26—Calendar Math

1. no
2. the 21st
3. five
4. Wednesday
5. Monday
6. Tuesday
7. Thursday
8. Wednesday
9. Tuesday
10. Tuesday

Brain Booster: Wednesday

## p. 27—Curious Coordinates

fish (5, 8)    puppy (3, 1)
snake (5, 5)   parrot (2, 6)
kitten (6, 3)  lizard (8, 7)
(1, 9) is the mouse
(9, 1) is the turtle

## p. 28—Hexagon Math

1. $1 + 1 = 2$
2. $3 + 2 = 5$
3. $3 \times 3 = 9$
4. $3 + 4 = 7$
5. $3 \times 5 = 15$
6. $2 + 4 = 6$
7. $5 \times 5 = 25$
8. $6 + 6 = 12$
9. $2 \times 2 = 4$
10. $1 \times 2 = 2$
11. $4 + 2 = 6$
12. $5 \times 2 = 10$

## p. 29—Tic-Tac-Toe Math

1. $2 - 2 = 0$
2. $6 \div 2 = 3$
3. $4 - 2 = 2$
4. $8 - 4 = 4$
5. $6 \div 3 = 2$
6. $10 \div 5 = 2$
7. $8 \div 2 = 4$
8. $9 - 3 = 6$
9. $12 \div 3 = 4$
10. $10 - 2 = 8$
11. $12 \div 2 = 6$
12. $12 \div 4 = 3$

## p. 30—Roll of the Dice

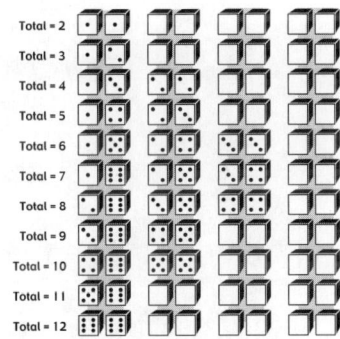

Total = 2
Total = 3
Total = 4
Total = 5
Total = 6
Total = 7
Total = 8
Total = 9
Total = 10
Total = 11
Total = 12

## p. 31—Numerical Path

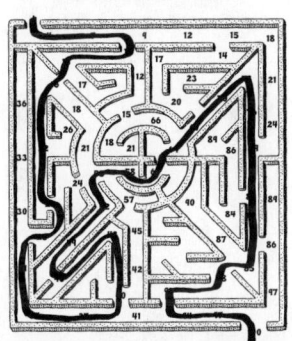

## p. 35—The Next Number
1. 17   23   30
2. 153   158   156
3. 768   3,072   12,288
4. 192   218   186
5. 73   108   150
6. 52   104   100
7. 1,392   1,537   1,482
8. 408   2,040   12,240

## p. 36—Marshmallow Madness
Answers will vary.

## p. 37—Flight Graph
Answers will vary.

## p. 64—Rapunzel Puzzle

# Mini Wind Chime

synthesis

Make a miniature wind chime. You will need: crepe paper, a cardboard tube (from a roll of toilet paper or paper towels), yarn, six or eight small jingle bells, scissors, a glue stick, and duct tape.

**1** Tear or cut crepe paper into bits. Glue to outside of the cardboard tube. Allow pieces to overlap, covering the entire tube.

**2** Cut three or four pieces of yarn that vary in length from 6 to 10" (15 to 25 cm). Thread three jingle bells on each piece of yarn, tying at intervals.

**3** Attach yarn inside tube with duct tape. Space evenly.

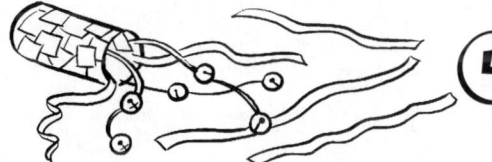

**4** Cut crepe paper streamers. Attach streamers inside tube with duct tape.

**5** Cut three pieces of yarn that are 8" (20 cm) long. Attach to the inside top of tube with duct tape. Space evenly. Tie together in a knot. Attach a longer piece of yarn to knot, and hang your wind chime.

**39**

synthesis

# Bedroom Mural

A mural is a painting that covers an entire wall. Ask an adult for permission to make a mural for your bedroom. You will need: butcher paper (or shelf paper), masking tape, crayons, markers, paint, scissors, construction paper, and old magazines.

**1** Cut sheets of paper as long as one wall. Tape corners and edges of paper to wall using masking tape.

**2** Plan out your mural in the space below. Create a flower garden, a forest filled with animals, or whatever you wish.

**3** Transfer your design to the paper on your wall. Decorate with crayons, markers, paint, paper cutouts, and magazine pictures. Use your imagination!

**40**

# Chenille Stem Sculptures

synthesis

These creative sculptures are fun to make. You will need: chenille stems (available at most craft stores), clay, scissors, newspaper, a drinking straw cut into pieces, and decorative items such as beads or pasta.

**1** Cover your work area with newspaper. Roll a lump of clay into a small ball about the size of your fist.

**2** Shape the clay to create the base of your sculpture.

**3** Use scissors to cut chenille stems into pieces. Bend into a variety of shapes. Press one end of each chenille stem into clay base.

**4** String decorative items on the chenille stems. Change or recreate your sculpture simply by bending chenille stems in different ways and adding new decorations.

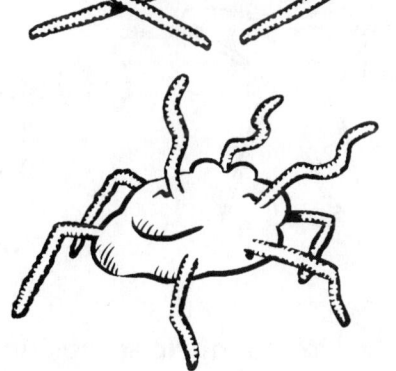

**Just for Fun:** Use clay and chenille stems to create more sculptures. Make creepy insects, scary aliens, or other strange creatures.

**41**

# Apple Head Doll

synthesis

Make a dried apple head doll. This project is easy to do but takes several weeks. You will need: one firm apple, lemon juice, one large paper clip, string, a wire hanger, and fabric scraps.

**1** Peel a large, firm apple. Using a peeler or knife, carve a face into the apple.

**2** Poke a large paper clip into the top of the apple. Attach to a string. Soak apple in lemon juice. Hang apple in a warm, dry area until it looks dry and shriveled (about 3–4 weeks).

**3** When your apple is dry, add hair and/or jewelry with yarn, fabric scraps, pins, or other materials.

**4** Straighten a wire hanger. Stick the apple head on the end. Bend the hanger to create a body. Try to make the doll able to stand on its own.

**5** Wrap fabric scraps and other materials around the wire frame to give your doll clothes. Add other finishing touches to make your doll complete. Be creative!

# Treasure Tin

 **A**

Make a keepsake tin. You will need: a rectangular gourmet coffee tin (or other small tin), gold and/or silver spray paint, a glue gun, and decorative trims such as "puff" paint pens (in squeeze bottles), glitter pens, sequins, beads, plastic gems, and aluminum foil balls.

**1** Wash and dry your tin.

**2** Ask an adult to help you spray paint the tin and lid with gold or silver paint. Let dry.

**3** Use the glue gun to attach any decorations and turn the can into a fancy treasure tin.

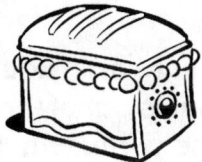
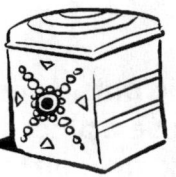

synthesis

# Let's Make a Luminaria

This glowing luminaria is fun and easy to make. You will need: a coffee can, a hammer, a nail, wrapping or construction paper, glue, and a votive candle.

**1** Wash out the coffee can with soap and water. Let dry.

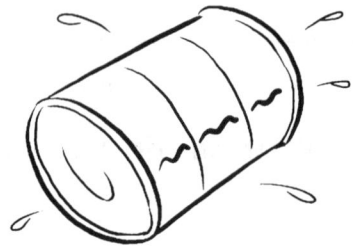

**2** Using a hammer and a nail, carefully punch holes in the can. Ask an adult for help. Create unique patterns or pictures with the holes.

**3** Glue decorative wrapping paper or brightly colored construction paper to the outside of the can.

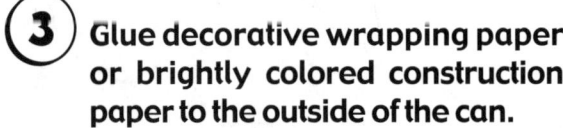

**4** Set a votive candle or tea light inside the can and light.

Set your luminaria outside at night or inside with the lights turned down. Choose a place that is out of the way, so no one will trip over it. Ask an adult to help you with this. Watch how the light shines through the holes in the side of the can.

# Quick & Easy Quilling

synthesis

In the fifteenth century, people rolled pieces of paper on bird quills to make beads. You can make colorful beads too. You will need: magazine pages, scissors, drinking straws, glue, and thin elastic or yarn.

**1** Cut magazine pages into long, thin triangles that measure 10" x 10" x 2" (25 cm x 25 cm x 5 cm).

**2** Roll the triangles around the end of a straw, beginning with the wide end. Put a drop of glue under the pointed tip to secure in place.

**3** Cut off the rest of the straw, leaving the section inside the bead for stringing.

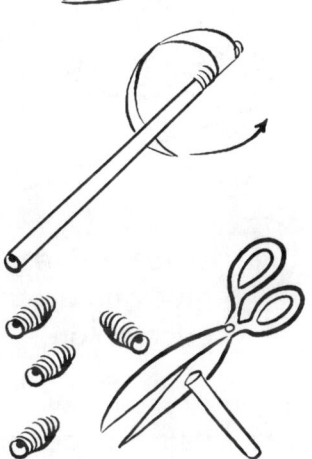

**4** When beads are dry, thread on short pieces of elastic to make bracelets or longer pieces of yarn to create necklaces. Tie ends into a knot and tuck under a bead.

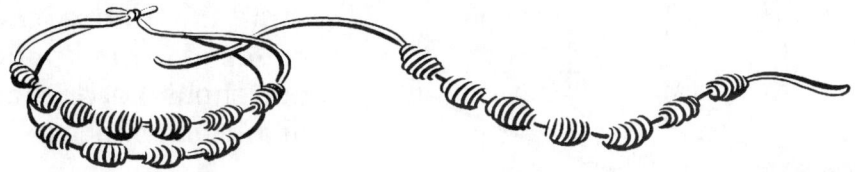

**45**

# Pebble Pencil Holder

synthesis

Make a pencil holder using your favorite pebbles and seashells. You will need: a juice can, small pebbles or seashells, tweezers or small pliers, and a glue gun.

**1** Wash juice can in warm, soapy water. Allow to dry completely.

**2** Wash pebbles and shells. Let dry.

**3** Trace a line of glue with a glue gun around the bottom edge of can.

**4** Using tweezers or small pliers, arrange pebbles and shells along line of glue. Let first row dry.

**5** Working upward, repeat until the entire can is covered with pebbles and shells. Let dry before filling with pencils.

IF0294 *Challenge Your Child*

# Make a Harp

synthesis

Create your own harp. You will need: water, a lemon, a ½ gallon (2 l) milk carton, white glue, adhesive shelf paper with woodgrain pattern (optional), a pencil, a craft knife or scissors, five thick rubber bands, and masking tape.

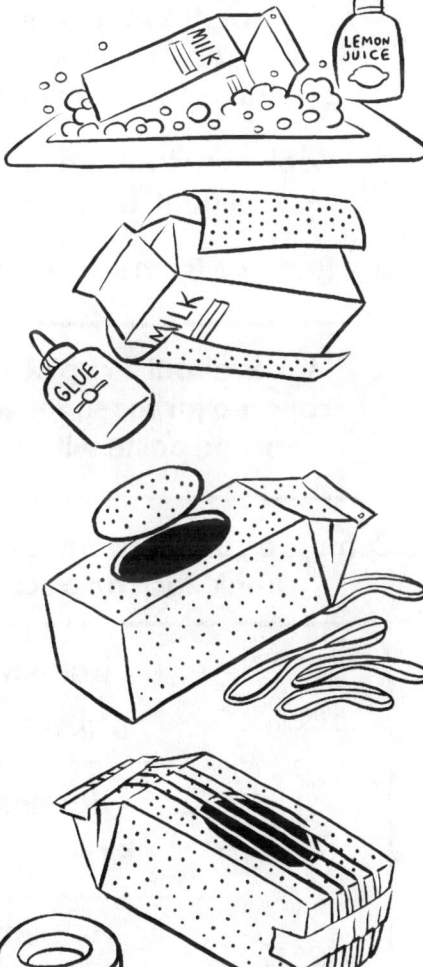

**1** Wash the milk carton in warm, soapy water. Rinse in lemon water (water with the juice of half a lemon). Let dry overnight.

**2** Glue the carton closed. If desired, cover carton with adhesive shelf paper.

**3** Make a paper circle or oval at least as wide as the five rubber bands. Place the circle or oval on one side of the carton and trace. Using scissors or a craft knife (ask an adult to help you), cut out the hole.

**4** Stretch the rubber bands the length of the carton across the hole. Space evenly and tape in position. Your harp is ready to play.

**47**

# Making Paste

You can make your own paste at home. You will need: ⅓ cup (79 ml) all-purpose wheat flour, 2 tablespoons (30 ml) sugar, ¼ teaspoon (1 ml) cinnamon, and 1 cup (237 ml) water.

**1** Mix flour, sugar, and cinnamon in saucepan. Gradually add water, stirring to break up lumps.

**2** Cook over low heat until clear, stirring constantly. (Ask an adult to supervise this step.)

**3** Remove from stove. Let cool. Store in a covered jar.

---

Makes about 1 cup (237 ml). Paste can be stored in a covered jar for several weeks without refrigeration. Spread paste with a brush or tongue depressor.

---

Compare your homemade glue with store-bought white glue. Rank each on a scale of 1 to 5, 1 being the best.

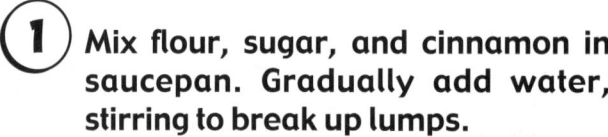

| | | | | | |
|---|---|---|---|---|---|
| **Homemade** | 1 | 2 | 3 | 4 | 5 |
| **Store bought** | 1 | 2 | 3 | 4 | 5 |
| **Homemade** | 1 | 2 | 3 | 4 | 5 |
| **Store bought** | 1 | 2 | 3 | 4 | 5 |
| **Homemade** | 1 | 2 | 3 | 4 | 5 |
| **Store bought** | 1 | 2 | 3 | 4 | 5 |

AROMA

STICKY

SMOOTH

# Recipe for Goop

evaluation

**A**

Goop is a fun and strange concoction that is easy to make. You will need: ½ cup (118 ml) white glue, ¾–1 cup (178–237 ml) cornstarch, and food coloring.

**1** Mix together craft glue and ¾ cup (178 ml) cornstarch in a disposable 1 pint (474 ml) container. Stir.

**2** When smooth, add a few drops of food coloring and stir.

**3** Knead mixture until smooth on a large, flat surface covered with newspaper. This will take a few minutes. If the mixture is too sticky, add 1 teaspoon (5 ml) cornstarch. If the mixture is too stringy, add ½ teaspoon (2 ml) glue.

**note:** Goop does not store well, so it should be used the day it is made. Be sure to clean up your mess when you are finished.

Answer the questions by coloring YES or NO.

Was the goop fun to make?     yes    no

Will you make it again?     yes    no

Will you tell your friends about it?     yes    no

Were the results surprising?     yes    no

**49**

synthesis

# Finger Paint Fun

Make your own finger paints. You will need: $^1/_2$ cup (118 ml) water, 1 tablespoon (15 ml) cornstarch, and food coloring.

**1** Combine water and cornstarch in a small, microwave-safe bowl. Microwave on **HIGH** for 30 seconds. Stir with wire whisk.

**2** Microwave on **HIGH** for another 30 to 90 seconds or until mixture starts to boil and thicken. Stir with wire whisk. Wearing oven mitts, carefully remove bowl from microwave.

**3** Pour mixture into three different bowls. Add food coloring to each bowl to make red, blue, and yellow paints. Stir to blend.

**4** Let paints cool to room temperature (about 10 minutes).

**5** Stir paint before using. Experiment with the primary colors to see which secondary colors (green, purple, orange) you can make.

For best results, use paint on wet, glossy shelf paper or wet finger painting paper. Paint with your fingers, paint-brushes, cotton swabs, or sponges.

# Modeling Dough

evaluation

You can make your own play dough in about 15 minutes. You will need: ¾ cup (178 ml) all-purpose flour, ½ cup (118 ml) salt, 1½ teaspoons (7 ml) powdered alum, 1½ teaspoons (7 ml) vegetable oil, ½ cup (118 ml) boiling water, and food coloring.

**(1)** Mix flour, salt, and alum in a large mixing bowl. Add oil and stir.

**(2)** Ask an adult to help you boil ½ cup (118 ml) water. Add boiling water to mixture. Stir vigorously with spoon. Dough should not stick to sides of bowl.

**(3)** Let dough cool before using.

Use your dough to make people, animals, and other shapes.
**Be creative!** Store unused dough in a jar with a tight lid.
Dough will keep several months without refrigeration.

| Rate your play dough on a 5-point scale, 5 being the best. | | | | |
|---|---|---|---|---|
| Smooth texture | 1 | 2 | 3 | 4 | 5 |
| Easy to work with | 1 | 2 | 3 | 4 | 5 |
| Hardens well | 1 | 2 | 3 | 4 | 5 |

# Chocolate Sandwich

synthesis

Make a tasty treat that is popular in France. You will need: French bread, a plain milk or dark chocolate bar, and a favorite beverage.

**1** Take a piece of French bread and place it on a plate. Tear the bread into chunks if desired.

**2** Put a piece of chocolate between two pieces of bread. Voilà! You have created a typical French child's favorite after-school snack.

**3** Wash down your snack with a tall glass of milk or water.

Rate your snack on a 5-point scale, 5 being the best.

| 1 | 2 | 3 | 4 | 5 |

**Just for Fun:** Try variations of the chocolate sandwich by adding one or more of these:

- chopped nuts
- sunflower seeds
- peanut butter
- raisins or other dried fruit
- apple or pear slices
- fresh berries

# Mango Salad

synthesis

 **A**

Make this tasty tropical fruit salad popular in Guyana. You will need: one mango, one banana, a handful of cherries, and sliced cashews.

**1** Wash and peel a ripe mango. The mango should be slightly soft to the touch and the skin will be red in color. Slice off small pieces of the fruit, working your way to the large seed in the mid-
d          l          e          .

**2** Peel and slice a banana. Add banana slices to the mango.

**3** Remove stems from cherries. Cut in half and remove pits. Add to the other fruits.

**4** Toss in some sliced cashews. Stir.

Rate the mango salad on a 5-point scale, 5 being the best.

| 1 | 2 | 3 | 4 | 5 |

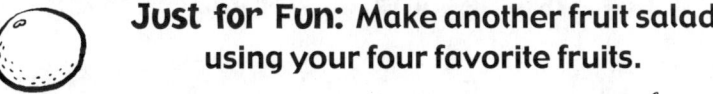

**Just for Fun:** Make another fruit salad using your four favorite fruits.

**53**

# Banana & Cheese Snacks

*evaluation*

Some children in Israel like to eat bananas with cheese. Do you? Read the snack variations below, then try them.

Read the recipes below before making the snacks. Which recipe sounds the best? Color your answer.

**(1)   (2)   (3)   (4)   (5)**

Choose one snack to prepare.

**(1)** Mash a peeled banana with a fork. Place the banana pulp between two slices of American cheese. Eat like a sandwich.

**(2)** Mix together grated cheddar cheese and a mashed banana. Spread on crackers and eat.

**(3)** Peel a banana and slice lengthwise. Top with cream cheese and sprinkle with powdered or brown sugar.

**(4)** Cut Monterey Jack cheese into small cubes. Cut a banana into thick slices. Alternate cheese cubes and banana slices on toothpicks.

**(5)** Melt a handful of Monterey Jack cheese cubes in the microwave (about 30 seconds). Dip banana chunks in the melted cheese. Eat with a toothpick.

Once you have tried all five variations, choose your favorite again. Color your answer. Is it the same answer you chose above?

 **(1)** **(2)** **(3)** **(4)** **(5)**

IF0294 *Challenge Your Child*

# Tortilla Sandwiches

synthesis

Tortillas are used in many Mexican dishes. Try making these three tortilla sandwiches at home.

## Quesadillas

Quesadillas are tortillas with melted cheese.
1. Butter a tortilla and put on a plate.
2. Sprinkle with grated cheese. Place another tortilla on top.
3. Microwave on **HIGH** for 30 seconds or until cheese melts. Cut like a pie and enjoy with salsa.

## Chicken Tacos

These soft tacos are easy to make.
1. Shred a cold, cooked chicken breast.
2. Place a tortilla on a glass plate.
3. Put shredded chicken on the tortilla.
4. Sprinkle with grated cheese.
5. Microwave on **HIGH** for 30 seconds or until cheese melts.
6. Add chopped lettuce and salsa.
7. Fold once and eat.

## Cinnamon Twists

For a sweet snack, make a cinnamon twist.
1. Butter a flour tortilla.
2. Sprinkle with sugar and cinnamon.
3. Roll up.
4. Microwave on **HIGH** for 30 seconds.

synthesis

# Chocolate Caramel Berries

This sweet treat is popular around the United States. You will need: strawberries, individually wrapped caramels, and a chocolate bar.

**1** Wash, dry, and slice enough strawberries to fill 1 cup (237 ml).

**2** Put several unwrapped caramels and a piece of chocolate bar in a glass bowl. Microwave on **HIGH** until melted. (You may substitute caramel and chocolate sauce or ice cream topping.)

**3** Pour chocolate and caramel mixture over strawberries. Let cool in refrigerator before eating.

Try topping strawberries with other tasty combinations.

Make a list of other things you think would taste good as dip or topping for fresh strawberries.

_____     _____

_____     _____

_____     _____

**56**

# Favorite Food Interview

synthesis

Ask a grandparent or other older relative to talk about a favorite food from his or her childhood. Fill out the recipe card. Then answer the questions below.

_____'s
### Favorite Dish

Name of Recipe: _____

Ingredients: _____

_____

_____

Directions: _____

_____

_____

_____

_____

1. Who used to make the dish for your relative?

_____

2. Was this dish made on special occasions or certain holidays?

_____

Ask your relative to help you make this dish. Serve to your family.

**57**

# The Grasshopper & the Ant

synthesis

"The Grasshopper and the Ant" is a fable about hard work. Read the fable below, then complete the activity.

There once was an ant that worked hard all summer storing food. Later that winter, as he was dragging out some grain for his supper, a grasshopper came along and asked for a bite to eat.

"Why do you come to me to be fed?" asked the ant. "What were you doing all summer while I slaved away storing food for the winter?"

The grasshopper smiled. "I spent the summer singing," he explained.

"Well," the ant replied, "you sang all summer, you can dance all winter."

Create your own grasshopper and ant figures using clay and chenille stems. Try to make your insects look as realistic as possible. Add your finished bugs to the diorama on page 59.

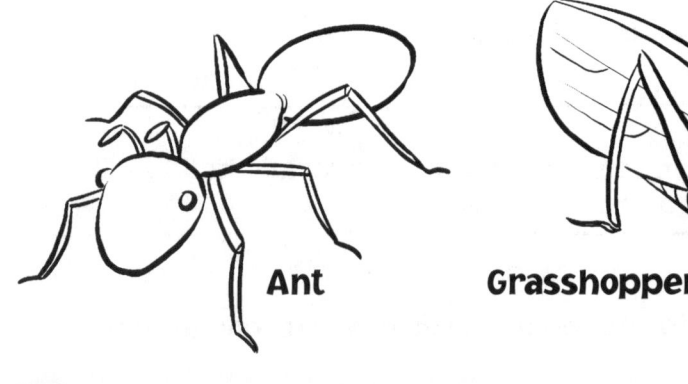

Ant          Grasshopper

IF0294 *Challenge Your Child*

# Dazzling Diorama

synthesis

Create a diorama of "The Grasshopper and the Ant."
You will need: a small cardboard box or shoe box,
paper, colored pencils or markers, sand, dirt, pebbles,
grass, twigs, and glue.

**1** Place the box on a sheet of paper. Trace around the bottom. Use this space to make a background for your diorama. Cut out the finished background and paste to the inside bottom of the box.

**2** Tip the box on its side with the opening facing you. Glue sand, dirt, grass, and other materials to the bottom of the diorama to represent the ground.

**3** Add small twigs and pebbles to create a 3-D effect.

**4** Add the ant and grasshopper you made on page 58.

**5** Use the diorama to tell the fable to friends and family.

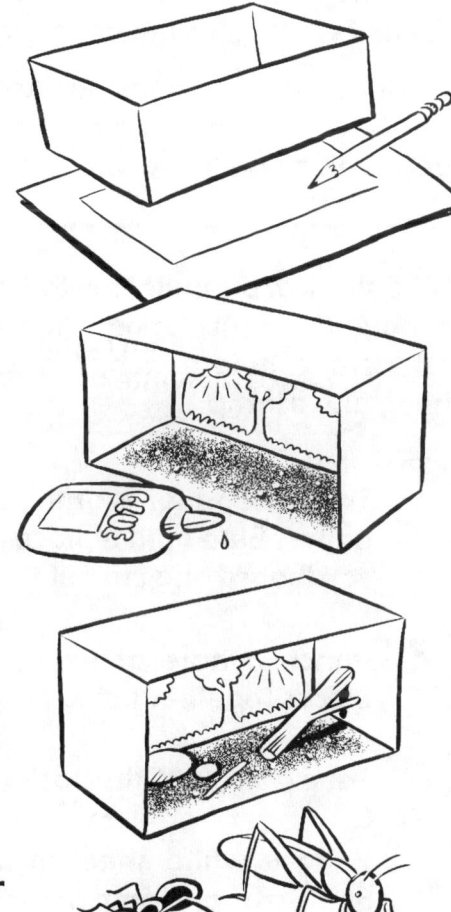

**59**

# The Golden Eggs

synthesis

"The Golden Eggs" is a fable about greed. Read the fable below, then complete the activity.

Once there was a farmer who owned a very special goose. The goose laid a single golden egg every day. The man grew richer each day, but he also became more and more greedy. He grew tired of waiting for the eggs to come one at a time.

Anxious for more eggs, the farmer cut open the goose one day. But the goose did not have any golden eggs inside her. The special goose died and the farmer was once again poor.

Make shadow puppets to retell the story. You will need: the patterns on page 61, white paper, lightweight cardboard, scissors, paper fasteners, a hole punch, masking tape, drinking straws, a white sheet, and a lamp.

**1** Trace the patterns onto a sheet of white paper. Glue onto a piece of lightweight cardboard and cut out.

**2** Punch a hole at each "X." Join the pieces together using paper fasteners.

**3** Tape a straw to the back of each piece.

**4** Hang a white sheet in a dark room. Shine a bright lamp onto one side of the sheet. Move the puppets between the lamp and the sheet. Your friends can watch the shadows from the other side of the sheet.

# Golden Patterns

synthesis

Use the patterns below to make shadow puppets. Follow the directions on page 60. Use your finished puppets to retell the story of "The Golden Eggs."

# More of the Golden Eggs

synthesis

Can you relate the story of "The Golden Eggs" to your own life? Have you ever wanted something so much that you could not wait for it?

Draw a picture of something you have wanted for a very long time.

Pretend you finally got what you most wanted. Write a story about getting the object but finding it disappointing. Start your story here. Use another sheet of paper if necessary.

_____

_____

_____

_____

_____

_____

_____

IF0294 *Challenge Your Child*

# Rapunzel

### Read the story of "Rapunzel."

comprehension

There once was a girl named Rapunzel, who was kept by a witch in a high tower in the middle of a deep forest. The tower had no door and only one small window near the very top. Every day the witch would come and say, "Rapunzel, Rapunzel, let down your golden hair." Rapunzel would undo her braids and let her long, flowing hair fall down through the window for the witch to climb.

Rapunzel was never allowed to leave the tower, and she grew very lonely. Like a nightingale, she would sing lonely songs all night long. One evening, a prince heard her singing as he rode his horse through the woods. Curious, he followed the sound to the tower and saw Rapunzel sitting at the window. Captured by her beauty, the prince decided to come back the very next day.

The prince returned to the tower the next morning. He hid behind a tree and watched as the witch called to Rapunzel and climbed up her tresses. After the witch had gone, the prince ran to the tower and called, "Rapunzel, Rapunzel, let down your golden hair." When she did, he climbed right up to the window. Though startled at first, Rapunzel soon grew fond of her kind visitor.

Rapunzel and the prince fell in love, and he came to visit her every night. One day, the witch found out about the prince. Angry, she cut off Rapunzel's hair and banned her to a remote desert. Then she hid in the tower and waited for the prince to return. When he called up to her, she let Rapunzel's hair fall as usual. As the prince reached the window, the witch pushed him to the ground where he was blinded by sharp thorns.

The prince wandered, lost for years, until one day he heard a familiar voice singing. It was Rapunzel. When she saw that he was blind, she cried. Two of her tears dropped on his eyes and magically restored his sight. The prince took her to his kingdom, where they were welcomed with great joy. The two of them lived happily ever after.

comprehension

# Rapunzel Puzzle

Number the pictures from 1 to 6 to show the correct order of the story.

# Spoon Puppets

synthesis

Make spoon puppets to retell the story of "Rapunzel." You will need: three plastic spoons, three chenille stems, black paper, yellow and black yarn, glue, and a black permanent marker with a fine tip.

## Rapunzel

1. Use yellow yarn to make a braid twice as long as the spoon. Fold over the top of the spoon and glue at the top so the braid hangs down on both sides. Glue a few short pieces of yellow yarn to make bangs.

2. Use the black marker to draw Rapunzel's face.

3. Wrap one chenille stem around the neck of the spoon and bend to look like arms.

## Witch

1. Cut short lengths of black yarn and tie them in the middle. Glue to the top of the second spoon.

2. Use the black marker to draw the witch's face.

3. Cut a small circle out of black paper. Cut a slit to the middle, and overlap to create a cone shape. Glue together and then glue on top of the witch's head.

4. Wrap one chenille stem around the neck of the spoon and bend to look like arms.

## Prince

Use your imagination to make the third spoon into a prince puppet. Then use all three puppets to tell the story to a friend or younger child.

synthesis

# Creating a Rhyme

*Deedle, deedle, dumpling, my son John,*
*Went to bed with his stockings on;*
*One shoe off, and one shoe on,*
*Deedle, deedle, dumpling, my son John.*

Change the words in the rhyme to create a poem about yourself. Begin by replacing the words "deedle" and "dumpling" with other two-syllable nonsense words. Then make sure the final words in lines four and six rhyme with your name.

_____, _____, _____,

I am _____ ,
(your name)

I went to _____ with

my _____

One _____,

and one _____,

_____, _____, _____,
(repeat first line)

I am _____ .
(your name)

**Just for Fun:** Now try writing a rhyme
for your best friend, brother, or sister.

IF0294 *Challenge Your Child*

# Plant Photo Album

analysis

Make a photo album of plants growing in your backyard or even inside your home. You will need: a camera (a disposable camera will do), a spiral notebook, rubber cement, and a pen or pencil.

**1** Take pictures of different plants growing in your yard or inside your home. For each plant, take two pictures: one of the whole plant and one of a leaf.

**2** Have the film developed, and look at your photos. Compare the plants with each other. How are they alike? How are they different? Compare your plants with the illustrations here. Can you identify the type of leaf in each of your pictures?

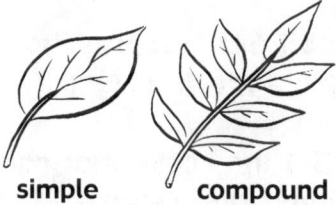

simple          compound

smooth     toothed     lobed

**3** Use rubber cement to mount your photos in a spiral note-book. You will need two pages per plant: one for the whole plant, and one for the leaf. Write the name of the plant beneath each picture, as well as other information you can gather about the plant and its leaves.

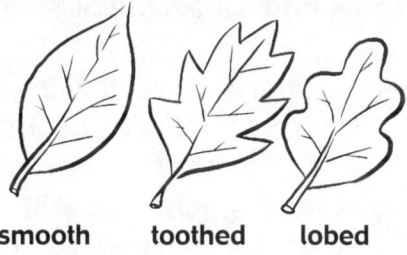

**67**

# Hard as a Rock

analysis

Go on a rock hunt. Can you find rocks that match the descriptions below? Check off each one you find.

_____ solid color
_____ mostly white
_____ mostly gray
_____ mostly black
_____ mostly brown
_____ partially red
_____ shiny
_____ striped

_____ big as a baseball
_____ smaller than a pea
_____ shaped like an egg
_____ looks like a sponge
_____ has a smooth fracture
_____ has a rough fracture
_____ has a flat surface
_____ feels powdery

Choose twelve different rocks from your collection. Use Mohs' scale to test the hardness of those rocks. You will need: a strong fingernail, a penny, and a steel file or scrap piece of glass.

**1** Scratch each rock with your fingernail. Set the rocks that can be scratched in a pile. Use the remaining rocks in step 2.

**2** Scratch each rock with a penny. Set the rocks that can be scratched in a pile. Use the remaining rocks in step 3.

**3** Scratch each rock with a steel file or piece of glass. Set the rocks that can be scratched in a pile. Use the remaining rocks in step 4.

**4** The remaining rocks should scratch the file or piece of glass.

**5** Now test the hardness within each pile of rocks. Rub two rocks together. The harder rock will scratch the other one. Continue until you can put all the rocks in order from softest to hardest.

# Floating a Needle

analysis

Can you get a needle to float on the surface of water? Grab a sewing needle and fill a bucket with water. Then try a variety of methods to make the needle stay afloat.

Did you succeed? If not, try following the directions below.

You will need: a sewing needle, a paper coffee filter, and a bucket of water.

1. Cut a square piece of coffee filter about as long as your thumb.
2. Place the needle on the filter and set on top of the water.
3. Watch. What happens to the filter?
4. What happens to the needle?

**Brain Booster:** Do you think this method would work for floating a person on water? Why or why not?

_____

_____

_____

# Does It Float?

synthesis

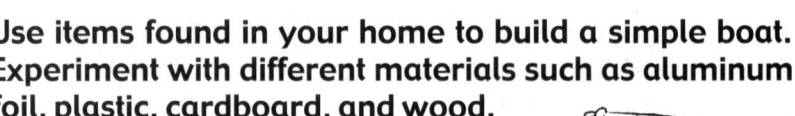

Use items found in your home to build a simple boat. Experiment with different materials such as aluminum foil, plastic, cardboard, and wood.

**1** Construct your boat, then test it in water. Fill a sink or dishpan with water. Set your boat on the surface of the water. Does it float? If not, adjust your design and try again. Keep trying until you have made a boat that floats.

**2** Sketch your boat design. List the supplies used to create it.

**Supplies:**

_____

_____

_____

_____

_____

_____

_____

_____

**3** Test the load your boat can carry. Set one large paper clip in the boat at a time. How many paper clips can your boat carry without sinking? _____

**Just for Fun:** Build a boat that can support an apple.

# Buried Time Capsule

synthesis

Create a time capsule to be opened in twenty years.

**1** Write a letter to your future adult self. Include the current date. Talk about your goals for the future and make six predictions.

**2** Include recent pictures of yourself with family and friends.

**3** Choose six more things to include in the time capsule. List them here.

1. _____   4. _____
2. _____   5. _____
3. _____   6. _____

**4** Put your letter, pictures, and other treasures in an airtight container. On the outside of the container, write the date it should be opened.

**5** Choose a safe place to bury your time capsule in your yard. You can even "bury" the time capsule inside your home—tuck it away in the basement, attic, or other storage space.

**Just for Fun:** Draw a map that will lead to your time capsule. Put the map in an envelope with the date you want to open it written on the outside. Ask a parent or other relative to keep it for you until that date.

**71**

# All About Seeds

analysis

> Seeds come in many shapes and sizes. Collect a variety of seeds from your kitchen or backyard. Spread them out on a sheet of paper. Answer the questions below.

1. What shape are most of the seeds? _____
2. Are the seeds all the same color or different colors? _____
3. Which seed is the most attractive? _____
4. Which seed has the most interesting shape? _____
5. Arrange the seeds from smallest to largest.
6. Arrange the seeds from roughest to smoothest.
7. Sort the seeds into two piles: colorful and not colorful.

Look at the pictures below. Different seeds travel in different ways. Can you find examples of each type of seed in your backyard?

**eaten and deposited by animals**

**carried by sticking to clothing or animals' fur**

**carried by wind**

**Just for Fun:** Use seeds to make a unique design or picture. Draw or paint an image, then add seeds using glue.

# Feeling Nature

comprehension

Create a guessing game using things you find in nature. You will need: a shoe box, scissors, and at least twelve of the items listed below.

- long blade of grass
- small branch
- smooth pebble
- pussy willow

- leaf
- moss
- acorn
- cattail

- fern frond
- berry
- snail's shell
- tuft of fur

- bird feather
- flower petal
- rough rock
- pinecone

**1** Cut a hole in the side of a shoe box. The hole should be large enough to fit your hand inside.

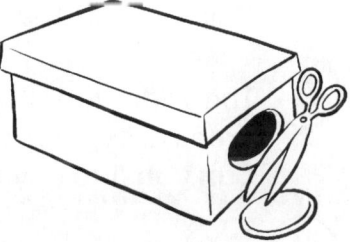

**2** Place the objects you have collected in the box. Cover the box with the lid.

**3** Reach inside the box and grab an object. Try to identify it. Remove each object as you identify it.

**4** Put the objects back in the box and challenge a friend to identify them.

analysis

# Birthday Party for a Tree

You can tell a lot about a tree by looking at its rings. Find a tree stump in your neighborhood or a favorite park.

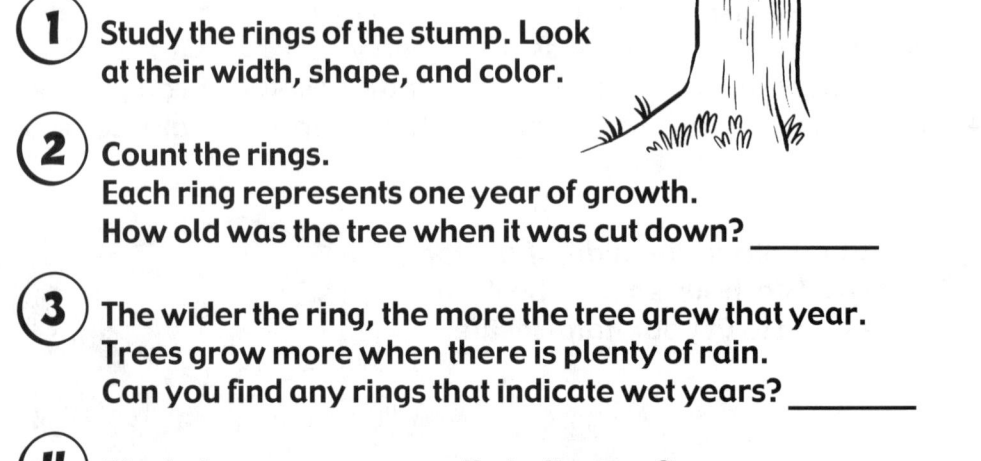

**1** Study the rings of the stump. Look at their width, shape, and color.

**2** Count the rings.
Each ring represents one year of growth.
How old was the tree when it was cut down? _____

**3** The wider the ring, the more the tree grew that year.
Trees grow more when there is plenty of rain.
Can you find any rings that indicate wet years? _____

**4** Black rings or scars usually indicate a fire.
Did the tree suffer any fire damage? _____

**5** A V-shaped notch in a ring indicates where a branch grew.
How many branches do you count in the 10th year? _____
20th year? _____

 Draw a picture of the stump below.
Try to draw the rings exactly as they appear.

# Nature's Paint Palette

knowledge

How many different colors can you find in your yard? Try to find one object that is each color below. As you find an example of each color, draw the object in the correct space.

| | | |
|---|---|---|
| red | pink | purple |
| green | brown | orange |
| blue | yellow | white |

Can you get a tic-tac-toe across, down, or diagonally?
Can you fill the entire board?

# A Square of Sod

knowledge

How many blades of grass grow in a small square of lawn? Find out! You will need: a butter knife, a spoon, a paper plate, and access to a lawn.

**1** Use a butter knife to cut around a 1" (25 mm) square of grass. Cut deep enough to reach the roots.

**2** Scoop out the sod with a spoon. If the sod is very dry, add a bit of water first. Shake off any excess soil.

**3** Place the sod on a paper plate.

## Answer the questions below.

1. How many blades of grass are there? _____

2. How many roots are there? _____

3. What is the average number of blades growing from each root? _____
(Hint: Divide the total number of roots by the total number of blades.)

4. How long is the tallest blade of grass? _____

5. How long is the shortest? _____

6. What is the difference in length? _____

7. How long do you think it will take for new grass to fill in the hole you dug? Watch and see.

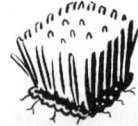

**Guess:** _____ days

**Actual:** _____ days

IF0294 *Challenge Your Child*